LIGHTNING BOLT BOOKS™

What Is Touch?

Jennifer Boothroyd

Lerner Publications Company
Minneapolis

For my husband, Don

Lerner Publications Company
A division of Lerner Publishing Group, Inc.
241 First Avenue North
Minneapolis, MN 55401 U.S.A.

Website address: www.lernerbooks.com

Library of Congress Cataloging-in-Publication Data

Boothroyd, Jennifer, 1972–
    What is touch? / by Jennifer Boothroyd.
        p.   cm. — (Lightning bolt books™—Your amazing senses)
    Includes index.
    ISBN 978–0–7613–4252–6 (lib. bdg. : alk. paper)
    1. Touch—Juvenile literature. I. Title.
    QP451.B66 2010
    612.8'8—dc22   2008051587

Manufactured in the United States of America
1 2 3 4 5 6 — BP — 15 14 13 12 11 10

Contents

Gathering Information

Have you ever petted a dog or a cat? What did the fur feel like?

What about a pet lizard or a turtle? How do those feel?

what something feels like by touching it.

You can tell what a starfish feels like by running your hand along its surface.

Touching is one of your five senses.

You use your skin to touch things.

You can tell what sand feels like by sifting it through your fingers.

Your sense of touch helps you learn about the world. It can also protect you from danger.

8

Your Skin and Nerves

You have thousands of nerves in your skin.

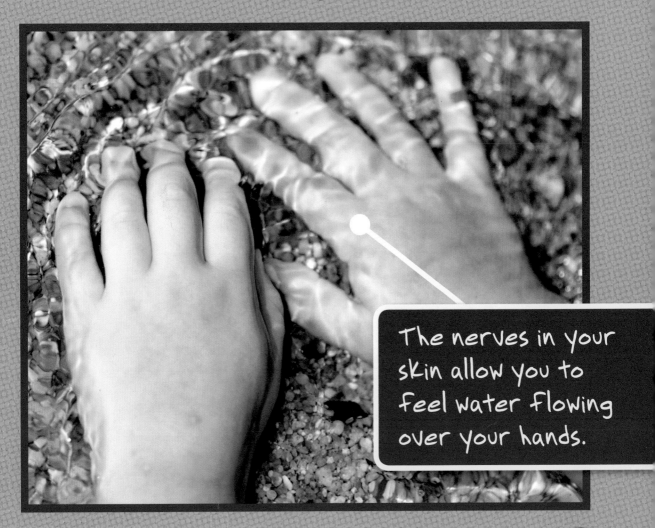

The nerves in your skin allow you to feel water flowing over your hands.

Your nerves can sense temperature, pain, pressure, and texture.

Nerves can detect the fuzzy texture of a peach.

The nerves send information about these things to your brain.

Your nerves send your brain all kinds of information about everything you touch.

11

Most people use their hands to touch.

Hands are perfectly designed for picking up objects—like this spiky sea urchin!

But you can touch things with your feet, your nose, or even your elbows because you have nerves all over your body.

Temperature

Your nerves can sense if something is hot or cold.

Thanks to your nerves, you can sense heat seeping through a mug.

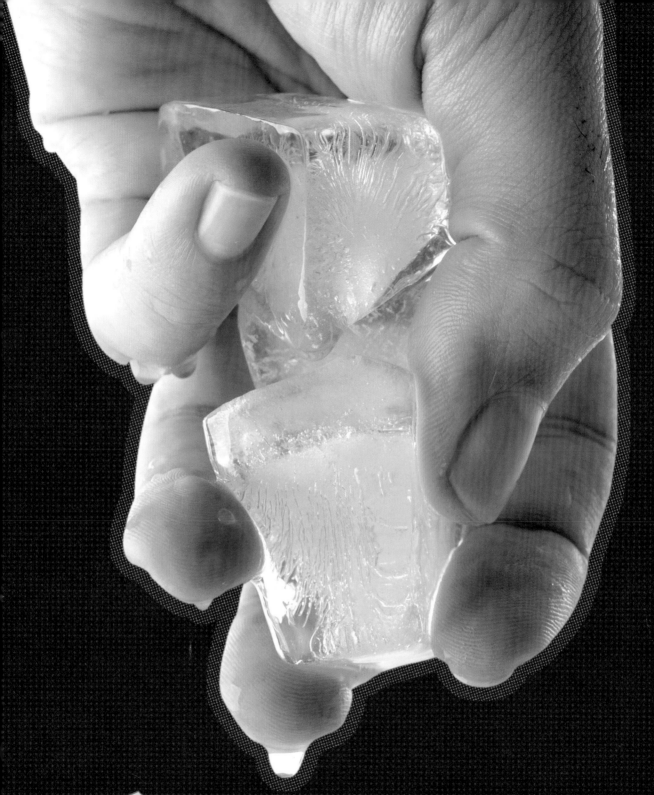

An ice cube is freezing.

Your forehead gets hot when you have a fever.

Pain

Some things we touch can cause us pain.

Look out! Touching a cactus can be painful.

17

Tight shoes can
pinch your toes.

A pan on the stove can burn you.

You should never touch a stove—or anything on a stove. Stoves can burn you even when you think they are turned off.

Your sense of pain tells you to stop. It keeps you from getting hurt even more.

Your sense of pain can warn you if a food is too hot to eat.

Pressure

Your skin feels pressure when something pushes on it.

Holding friends' hands puts pressure on your skin.

You feel squeezed when your grandpa gives you a big hug.

You can feel it when your grandma kisses your cheek.

Texture

Your skin can also feel texture.

A burlap sack has a very rough texture.

Some rocks are smooth, and others are rough.

Pajamas are soft.
A wool sweater is scratchy.

Flannel pajamas and fluffy pillows have a soft, smooth texture.

26

Touching is an important sense. You use it every day.

Test Your Sense of Touch

Ask an adult if you can try this experiment to test your sense of touch.

What you need:

a friend or classmate to work with
any four of the following items:

> a metal spoon
> a plastic spoon
> a bar of soap
> steel wool
> a sponge
> a piece of satin fabric
> a piece of cotton fabric

a box (about the size of a
  shoe box)
a cloth to use as a blindfold
rubber dishwashing gloves

What you do:

1. Show your friend each of your four items.

2. Place the items in the box.

3. Tie the cloth around your friend's eyes.

4. One by one, ask your friend to pull each item from the box. Be specific. Ask for the piece of cotton fabric or the metal spoon.

5. Put the objects back in the box and have your friend put on the pair of rubber dishwashing gloves.

6. Try the experiment again. Is it more difficult this time?

If you want, you can try switching roles to see if you can pull each item from the box. You can also try using different items. Are some items harder to identify than others?

Glossary

nerve: a thin fiber that sends messages between your brain and other parts of your body

pressure: a force caused by one thing pushing against another thing

sense: one of the powers that people and animals use to learn about their surroundings. The five senses are sight, hearing, touch, taste, and smell.

temperature: the degree of heat or cold in something

texture: the feel of something—especially its roughness or smoothness

Further Reading

Enchanted Learning: Five Senses Theme Page
http://www.enchantedlearning.com/themes/
senses.shtml

Gordon, Sharon. *Touching.* New York: Children's Press, 2001.

Haddon, Jean. *Make Sense!* Minneapolis: Millbrook Press, 2007.

Hewitt, Sally. *Touch That!* New York: Crabtree, 2008.

Kids Health: How the Body Works
http://kidshealth.org/kid/htbw

Rotner, Shelley. *Senses on the Farm.* Minneapolis: Millbrook Press, 2009.

Index

Photo Acknowledgments

The images in this book are used with the permission of: © James Cotier/The Image Bank/ Getty Images, p. 1; © Ricky John Molloy/Digital Vision/Getty Images, p. 2; © John Howard/ Lifesize/Getty Images, p. 4; Reflexstock/Corbis, p. 5; © Michele Westmoreland/DanitaDelimont .com, p. 6; © Cbeckwith/Dreamstime.com, p. 7; © Ale Ventura/Photoalto/Photolibrary, p. 8; © Olga/sweet/Dreamstime.com, p. 9; © Lynne Styler Photography/Alamy, p. 11; © Holger Hill/ Fstop/Getty Images, p. 12; © Ryan McVay/Lifesize/Getty Images, p. 13; © Brooke Slezak/Getty Images, p. 14; © Vtupinamba/Dreamstime.com, p. 15; © Tom Le Goff/Digital Vision/Getty Images, p. 16; © James Cotier/The Image Bank/Getty Images, p. 17; © iStockphoto.com/Nancy Louie, p. 18; © Kelpfish/Dreamstime.com, p. 19; © iStockphoto.com/Rhienna Cutler, p. 20; Reflexstock/Corbis/© Royalty-Free/Corbis, p. 21; © Barbara Penoyar/Photodisc/Getty Images, p. 21; © Paul Burns/Digital Vision/Getty Images, p. 22; © Ebbie May/Taxi/Getty Images, p. 24; © Sami Sarkis/Photographers Chioce RF/Getty Images, p. 25; Reflexstock/Image Source/ © Image Source Royalty-Free, p. 26; © BLOOMimage/Getty Images, p. 27; © Todd Strand/ Independent Picture Service, p. 28; © iStockphoto.com/Igor Profe, p. 30; © Lisa Sciascia/ fstop/Getty Images.

Front cover: © Todd Strand/Independent Picture Service.